Religions of the World

Hinduism

Rita Faelli

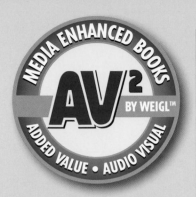

MEDIA ENHANCED BOOKS
AV²
BY WEIGL™
ADDED VALUE • AUDIO VISUAL

AV² provides enriched content that supplements and complements this book. Weigl's AV² books strive to create inspired learning and engage young minds in a total learning experience.

Your AV² Media Enhanced books come alive with...

Audio
Listen to sections of the book read aloud.

Key Words
Study vocabulary, and complete a matching word activity.

Video
Watch informative video clips.

Quizzes
Test your knowledge.

Go to **www.av2books.com**, and enter this book's unique code.

BOOK CODE

S674558

Embedded Weblinks
Gain additional information for research.

Slide Show
View images and captions, and prepare a presentation.

AV² by Weigl brings you media enhanced books that support active learning.

Try This!
Complete activities and hands-on experiments.

... and much, much more!

Published by AV² by Weigl
350 5ᵗʰ Avenue, 59ᵗʰ Floor
New York, NY 10118
Website: www.av2books.com

Library of Congress Control Number: 2015942086

ISBN 978-1-4896-4031-4 (hardcover)
ISBN 978-1-4896-4032-1 (soft cover)
ISBN 978-1-4896-4033-8 (single user eBook)
ISBN 978-1-4896-4034-5 (multi-user eBook)

Printed in the United States of America in Brainerd, Minnesota
1 2 3 4 5 6 7 8 9 0 19 18 17 16 15

052015
052215

Photo Credits

The publisher gratefully acknowledges the photo suppliers for this title: iStock, pages 1, 5; Vera Bogaerts, page 4; MAPgraphics, page 6; Ravi Tahilramani, page 7; Experience Foundation, page 9; Rohrt Seth, page 15; Kabir Baskie, p. 22; Shasti Kochhar, pages 23, 26; Melanie Taylor, page 24. All other photographs and illustrations are © copyright UC Publishing Pty Ltd.

Every reasonable effort has been made to trace ownership and to obtain permission to reprint copyright material. The publishers would be pleased to have any errors or omissions brought to their attention so that they may be corrected in subsequent printings.

First published in 2006 by Blake Publishing
Copyright © 2006 Blake Publishing

Contents

What Is Hinduism?

Hinduism is one of the oldest religions in the world. It evolved over thousands of years in India. People who follow Hinduism are called Hindus. Another name for Hinduism is *Sanatana Dharma* – the Eternal Way.

Hinduism is based on the ancient religious traditions of India. It is made up of many different beliefs and practices. Unlike most world religions, it does not have a founder.

Word fact

The word Hindu was introduced by British writers in about 1830. It comes from their name for the people who lived near the Indus River in India.

Hinduism has many gods and goddesses. Vishnu helps protect the Earth and maintain its balance of good and evil.

Hindus in the World

About 900 million people follow Hinduism. Most Hindus live in India and in the nearby countries. However, there are Hindus all over the world.

About 1,000 years ago, traders took Hinduism to Malaysia, Thailand and other parts of South-East Asia. In more recent times, Hindus have migrated to the rest of the world, including Europe, America, Canada and Australia.

Hindu Beliefs

Hindus are taught to live a life of duty and good behavior. This is called **dharma**.

For Hindus, dharma means that they must worship God, work hard and not hurt other people and animals. They must think of others first and respect their parents, teachers and elders.

Hindus are very accepting of different ways of worship. They do not try to **convert** other people to their religion.

> **Fast fact**
> Hindus greet each other by joining their hands and saying **namaste**, or by touching their elders' feet.

Rebirth and Karma

Two important beliefs for Hindus are rebirth and **karma**.

Hindus believe that when you die your soul is reborn into another body. How you are reborn is based on the law of karma. Doing good things in this life will help a person to be reborn to a better life next time.

Fast fact

The Indian city of Varanasi is said to be a special place. Some Hindus believe that if you die there you will go straight to Heaven.

Meditation and Yoga

Many Hindus meditate and practise **yoga** as part of their worship.

Meditation is when someone sits quietly and thinks only about a special word or picture. Yoga is a series of exercises and breathing techniques. Meditation and yoga help people to become peaceful and calm.

Fast fact

Some Hindus meditate by concentrating on a **yantra**, which is a special design or pattern.

Respect for Life

Hindus believe that all life is sacred. They try to avoid mental, emotional and physical injury to all beings, human and animal. This is called **ahimsa**, or nonviolence.

Hindus do not believe in killing animals to eat. Because of this, many Hindus are **vegetarians**. A vegetarian is a person who has a diet of fruit, vegetables, cereals, pulses, nuts, sugar, honey, milk, and milk products.

Fast facts

- Hindus wash their hands and rinse their mouths before and after each meal.

- Hindus do not consume food or drink that has been tasted or sampled by another person.

Mahatma Gandhi

Mahatma Gandhi is a famous example of a Hindu leader who practised nonviolence. He was born in 1865 and died in 1948.

At this time, Great Britain ruled India. Gandhi led the struggle for India to become independent of British rule.

Gandhi did not believe in fighting or using violence. He told Indians that they could gain their freedom through peaceful means.

The teachings of Gandhi have inspired other nonviolent movements elsewhere. One example is the **civil rights movement** in the United States, led by people such as Martin Luther King, Jr.

Hindu Holy Books

The oldest Hindu sacred books are called the ***Vedas***. Vedas means knowledge.

The Vedas teach Hindus about how they should live and their responsibilities to the family and community. They also have instructions about the right way to worship and how ceremonies should be performed.

Having thus spoken of the Yogī follownig t
stage of his Sādhanā in the shape of seeing unity
the final stage of Sādhanā of a follower of the pa
in every being:—

यो मां पश्यति सर्वं च
तस्याहं न प्रणश्यामि स च मे

य: who; सर्वत्र (present) in all beings; माम् M
He is called); पश्यति sees; च and; सर्वम् the totalit
Universal Self or Vāsudeva); पश्यति sees; तस्य to
of sight; च and; स: he; मे to Me; न प्रणश्यति nev

He who sees Me (the Universal Self) presen
within Me, never loses sight of Me, and I ne

Just as ether exists in the cloud, and the   bei
cloud in ether even so God is   her

Fast fact

The Vedas are written in an ancient Indian language called **Sanskrit**.

12

Brahman

Most Hindus believe in a supreme power, or God. They call this power **Brahman**.

Hindus believe that Brahman created the universe and is present in everything – in people, animals, and plants.

Hindus can think of Brahman in any form that they choose. Some think of Brahman in the form of a person or animal.

Fast fact
Some Hindus use fire as a symbol of Brahman. This is because fire is seen as pure.

Gods and Goddesses

Hinduism has many gods and goddesses. Each one represents a different form and aspect of Brahman.

Vishnu is the protector of the universe. He appeared on earth to save humans from natural disasters or from tyranny. ▶

◀ Shiva is the destroyer. Shiva is the source of both good and evil. Although he can be a frightening god, he is also a kind god.

Lakshmi is Vishnu's wife. ▶
She is the goddess of
beauty, wealth,
and prosperity.

◀ A very popular god is
Ganesha, the son of Shiva
and Parvati. Ganesha is
the god of wisdom and
education. He is also the
remover of obstacles.

Parvati is Shiva's wife.
She is known as the
Mother Goddess. ▶

Where Do Hindus Worship?

Temples are special places where Hindus can visit and worship their gods.

A temple is considered to be the house of a god or goddess on earth.

Fast fact

At a Hindu temple, different parts of the building have different meanings. The central **shrine** is a symbol of the worshipper's heart. The tower represents the flight of the spirit to heaven.

A typical Hindu temple consists of:

- an entrance, often with a porch
- one or more halls, either attached to the main building or separate
- an inner **sanctum**
- a tower, built directly above the inner sanctum.

Before entering a temple, people must take off their shoes. This is a sign of respect to the temple's gods and goddesses. It also helps to keep the temple clean.

Inside the temple is a shrine. At the shrine's centre is a statue of the god, goddess, or a holy person to whom the temple is dedicated.

This statue is called a **murti**. In some shrines there may be a picture instead of a murti.

Hindus can visit the temple whenever they like. There is no set time for worship in a temple.

Hindus visit the temple to offer special food or gifts to their favorite god or goddess in the shrine. They receive blessings and can pray, sing and chant from the sacred books.

How Do Hindus Worship?

Hindu worship is called **puja**. It involves images of deities, prayers and yantras.

Worship can be carried out in a temple or in the home shrine. Worshippers repeat prayers and the names of their favorite gods and goddesses and make **offerings**.

Offerings are the special gifts given to the gods. They are usually fruit, flowers, incense and red and yellow colored powders.

Pujas are performed at various times during the day. In the temple, the priest takes the offerings from the people and offers them to the god to be blessed.

After the offerings are blessed, the priest gives them back to the worshippers. In this way, the god's blessing goes back to the worshippers. Sometimes the food offerings are shared among the people who are at the temple.

Worship at Home

For many Hindus, their own home is an important place to worship. Hindus make a special place in their home for a family shrine.

The shrine can be in a special room, or just a special space, such as a shelf or corner in a room.

A statue or picture of the family god or goddess is placed at the centre of the shrine. It is surrounded by the different personal deities of family members.

Hindu Priests

Hindu priests are men who have given up their home and belongings to lead a life of prayer and **meditation**.

Each temple is looked after by a priest, who performs the puja ceremony. It is the priest's job to visit families and to conduct different ceremonies for when a baby is born, or when there is a wedding or a funeral.

Symbols

Two important Hindu symbols are the aum and the tilaka.

Aum

The most important symbol in Hinduism is the aum symbol. It is made up of three Sanskrit letters: aa, au and ma. Together they make the sound aum (pronounced ah-oo-m). Hindus believe that this is the sound that God made at the creation of the universe.

Tilaka

The tilaka is drawn in the centre of the forehead. It is usually made with clay, ashes or sandalwood. People wear a tilaka as a mark of devotion to the Hindu gods.

Childhood Ceremonies

Hindus call the different stages of life **samskaras**. There are eight special ceremonies that mark the different stages of childhood.

When Hindu babies are born, they are welcomed into the family. Some honey is put in the child's mouth and the name of God is whispered in the child's ear.

Other rituals celebrate naming the baby, the child's first outing and first taste of solid food. Getting your ears pierced and your hair cut for the first time are also very important occasions.

Hindu Weddings

An important life stage is marriage. It is celebrated in the Hindu wedding ceremony, which can be very elaborate.

As well as being important social occasions, Hindu weddings include many religious **rites**.

Fast fact
One wedding tradition is that the groom, dressed in beautiful clothes, travels to the wedding site on a white mare.

Death

The last samskara is when a person has died and has been cremated.

After the death of a family member, relatives perform various ceremonies. For most Hindus, cremation is preferred. Hindus believe fire is clean and pure. They believe cremation will purify the dead body.

After a cremation, the ashes are collected and usually scattered in running water.

Fast fact

The River Ganges in India is considered the most sacred place to scatter the ashes from a cremation.

Hindu Festivals

Hindus celebrate many religious festivals throughout the year. Festivals are happy and lively times. Family and friends come together to join in the celebrations.

Some festivals celebrate the birthdays of gods and goddesses or important events that have happened in their lives. Other festivals celebrate events that happen when the seasons change, like harvest time.

One important festival is **Diwali**, the Festival of Lights. It is a four-day festival, falling in October or November.

At Diwali, people light small, clay lamps and candles and place them by their doors and windows. They also clean their houses during this time.

Diwali is a special time for remembering Lakshmi, the goddess of good fortune and wealth, and the victory of goodness over evil.

Word fact
Diwali means row of lamps.

Key Words

ahimsa nonviolence

Brahman Hindu name for God

civil rights movement 1960s movement for racial equality in the United States

convert persuade someone to change to a different religion

dharma Hindu life of duty and good behavior

Diwali a four-day festival, falling in late October or early November and celebrated by displaying lights and worshipping the goddess Lakshmi

karma the belief that how you behave affects this life and future lives

Lakshmi Hindu goddess of beauty, wealth and prosperity

meditation practice of clearing your mind of thoughts and feelings for religious reasons

murti a statue or picture of a god or goddess, used by Hindus during worship

namaste Hindu greeting

offerings special gifts given to the gods

puja Hindu worship

rites ceremonies that are always performed in the same way

samskaras stages of life

sanctum private place or room

Sanskrit ancient Indian language

shrine special room or area in a room for worship

temples special buildings of worship

Vedas the oldest Hindu sacred books

vegetarians people who do not eat meat

Vishnu Hindu god, the protector of the universe

yantra a special design or pattern that Hindus use to help them meditate

yoga a series of mental and physical exercises

Index

Log on to www.av2books.com

AV² by Weigl brings you media enhanced books that support active learning. Go to www.av2books.com, and enter the special code found on page 2 of this book. You will gain access to enriched and enhanced content that supplements and complements this book. Content includes video, audio, weblinks, quizzes, a slide show, and activities.

AV² Online Navigation

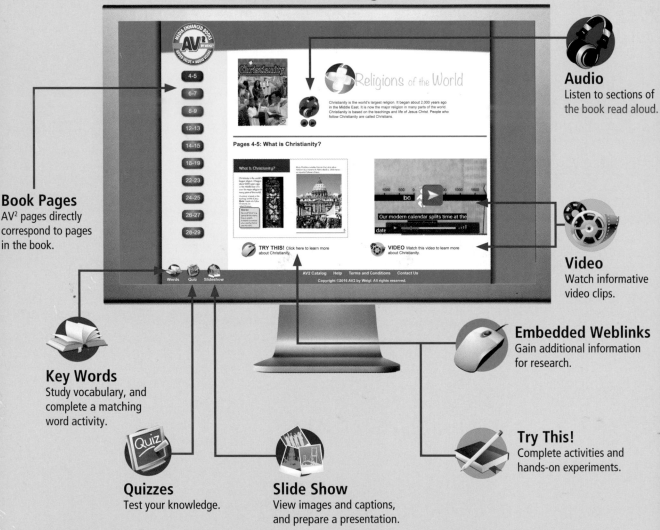

Audio
Listen to sections of the book read aloud.

Book Pages
AV² pages directly correspond to pages in the book.

Video
Watch informative video clips.

Key Words
Study vocabulary, and complete a matching word activity.

Embedded Weblinks
Gain additional information for research.

Quizzes
Test your knowledge.

Slide Show
View images and captions, and prepare a presentation.

Try This!
Complete activities and hands-on experiments.

AV² was built to bridge the gap between print and digital. We encourage you to tell us what you like and what you want to see in the future.

Sign up to be an AV² Ambassador at www.av2books.com/ambassador.